Working Together Against
HATE GROUPS

People throughout the world are fighting against hate groups like neo-Nazis.

❖THE LIBRARY OF SOCIAL ACTIVISM❖

Working Together Against

HATE GROUPS

Rose Blue
and Corrine J. Naden

THE ROSEN PUBLISHING GROUP, INC.
NEW YORK

Published in 1994 by The Rosen Publishing Group, Inc.
29 East 21st Street, New York, NY 10010

First Edition

Library of Congress Cataloging-in-Publication Data

Blue, Rose.
   Working together against hate groups / by Rose Blue and Corrine J.
Naden.
      p.   cm. — (Library of social activism)
   Includes bibliographical references (p.   ) and index.
   ISBN 0-8239-1776-2
   1. Minorities—Crimes against—United States—Prevention—Juvenile
literature. 2. Hate crimes—United States—Prevention—Juvenile
literature. [1. Hate crimes. 2. Prejudices.] I. Naden, Corinne J.
II. Title. III. Series.
HV6250.4.E75B58   1994
364.1—dc20   94-433
                                                 CIP
                                                 AC

Manufactured in the United States of America

Contents

INTRODUCTION

ON A FALL NIGHT IN PORTLAND, OREGON, IN 1988, a student from Ethiopia named Mulugeta Seraw was being dropped by some friends. The fact that Seraw and his friends were African was enough reason for a passing carload of racist Skinheads to stop, honk their horn, and yell at them. When the African men responded with an obscene gesture, the Skinheads seized on this excuse to fight. They jumped out of their car and began to break the other car's windows with a baseball bat. An African man and one of the Skinheads began to fight, but the African man managed to get away. Meanwhile, Seraw was being beaten with a baseball bat.

At the trial, Steve Strasser, one of the Skinheads, described how Seraw had fallen over and begun "a really freaky kind of yelling. . . It was like crying death. It's something you'd never forget." The Skinhead, Ken Mieske, who dealt the blow that killed Seraw, is now serving a life term for murder.

What is frightening about the murder of

Mulugeta Seraw is not simply that it happened, or even the horrible way that it happened. What should frighten all of us is that acts of hate, racism, and bigotry like this continue to happen, and that they happen everywhere. These crimes are committed by individuals, and by groups. Groups of people united by prejudice against other groups are known as hate groups. Skinheads are an example of a hate group. Hate groups have existed for a long time, and unfortunately, unless people take a stand against them, they will continue to exist.

Why should you care about hate groups? Because hate group activity affects everyone. Hate groups publish literature which is seen by many people. They buy airtime on radio and TV to spread their message. They have candidates for political offices. By using the media, and by becoming more involved with other political groups, as well as certain religious groups, hate groups have acquired a national influence.

Hate groups are dangerous, too.

❖ QUESTIONS TO ASK YOURSELF ❖

Hate affects everyone, from black to white, Jewish to Muslim, small towns to big cities. Think about how it affects you. 1) Have you ever heard a racist or an ethnic joke? Have you ever been the butt of one? 2) How did either situation make you feel?

No one is born with hatred and intolerance. They are taught at an
early age by others.

chapter

1

THE PROBLEM OF HATE GROUPS

THE KU KLUX KLAN. ARYAN NATIONS. Chicago White Vikings. Church of the Creator. National Association for the Advancement of White People. Identity. Bomber Boys.

These odd-sounding names belong to groups who hate other people because of their race, ethnic origin, religion, sexual orientation, gender, or political beliefs. Often their hate turns to violence. These groups are known as white supremacist groups because they believe the white race is superior to all others. Their hatred of people who do not belong to the white race is the reason they are called hate groups.

Today there are about 350 known white supremacist groups in the United States; and other groups exist in Europe as well. It is believed about 5,000 Americans are members of the Ku Klux Klan, and about 17,000 Americans belong to other racist organizations. These organizations target people who do not fit into

Some hate groups want racial segregation.

their picture of an ideal society. Their targets
vary. In white neighborhoods, it may be the
one black family. In minority communities, the
leaders become targets. Hate groups are responsible for murders, bombings, arson, assaults,
threats, cross burnings, harassment, vandalism,
and other crimes. They hold marches, rallies,
conventions, meetings, and distribute literature.

The Church of the Creator is a white
supremacist group. Its leader, Ben Klassen, says:
"We want a country rid of Jews and Blacks." In
Klassen's office is a large picture of Adolf Hitler,
whom he calls "the greatest leader the white

race ever had." Klassen trains young men, often teenagers, to handle automatic weapons in his church compound, where they have firing ranges and paramilitary barracks.

The Church of the Creator is like many other hate groups in that it promotes violence. It collects weapons and explosives and conducts paramilitary training. Skinheads' main weapons are baseball bats and the steel-toed combat boots they wear. Hate groups have wild and extreme plans for violence. A group of eight people were arrested in Los Angeles in 1993 because they planned to kill the members of the rap group Public Enemy, and also Rodney King.

The Church of the Creator targets young people for membership. So do Youth for Hitler, Youth Defense League, White Youth League, and United Aryan Youth. In 1979, twelve teenagers wearing Ku Klux Klan costumes burned an old school bus while Klan members cheered. Children have been taught how to use weapons at a Klan training camp in Alabama.

❖ QUESTIONS TO ASK YOURSELF ❖

Hate groups promote racist beliefs through violence and recruitment. Everyone is a target for recruiting. 1) How would you react if you were approached by a member of the Ku Klux Klan or Youth for Hitler?

Germany's Nazi Party, led by Adolf Hitler, murdered millions of people that Hitler deemed worthless, including Jews, gypsies, and homosexuals.

chapter

2

FACTS ABOUT HATE GROUPS

THE KU KLUX KLAN, AMERICA'S BEST KNOWN hate group, is still the one that most people know about. It was formed in the Reconstruction period after the Civil War, by poor white southerners and ex-slave owners. Their object was to control through intimidation and murder, the elected black leaders, and important local black persons.

In their white robes and pointed caps, Klansmen appeared during the night at black homes, to threaten, murder, and set fires. More and more assaults, robberies and murders were committed by Klan members. Congress passed an anti-Klan law.

After white people gained control of most Southern states, the clan diminished in numbers and in power.

The Klan was not dead for long, however. The Klan has risen again several times to terrorize minorities in the United States. It is not a coincidence that the Klan has become more powerful at exactly those times in history when social changes are taking place. The Klan has been able to increase people's fears about immigrants and civil rights for all. By wrongly convincing people that these kinds of changes are dangerous, the Klan is able to attract new members and become more violent in its activities.

❖ DIFFERENT HATE GROUPS ❖

There are many different hate groups across the United States and around the world. A group called Klanwatch, in Montgomery, Alabama, does an excellent job of keeping track of hate groups—and where they are located. Here are some hate groups.

- **Identity** is a hate group which misrepresents itself as a religious group and has "churches" in 33 states as well as in Canada, England, South Africa and Australia. Identity puts out the false message that Jewish people are descendants of Satan and that only white Anglo-Saxons are God's chosen people.
- **Separatists**, also known as **Nationalists**, mistakenly believe that whites should have

their own separate nation and minorities should have theirs.

- **Third Position**, says the government "has too many Jews and other enemies of whites."
- **Racial Survivalists** believe in war, and maintain that there will be a war between the races. To prepare for this war, racial survivalists often live in communes. They stockpile weapons and practice using them.
- **Anti-Native American** groups mistakenly believe that Native Americans are given special privileges. Even though they are clearly based on racism, anti-Native American hate groups claim that they are simply supporting equality for everyone. They have misleading names, such as **"Interstate Congress for Equal Rights and Responsibilities"**, and **"Protect Americans' Rights and Resources."** These groups have been shown to be connected with white supremacist groups. An example of anti-Native American hate group activity occurred in Wisconsin in 1988, when a group tried to prevent traditional Chippewa spearfishing by throwing pipe bombs, slashing tires and firing rifles when the Chippewa tried to exercise their right to spearfish.

❖ DO ONLY WHITES HATE? ❖

So far, all of the groups discussed here have been white supremacist groups, but there are people besides whites who hold racist beliefs, and who spread a message of hatred against people who are different from themselves. Fourteen members of a religious cult called the Yahwehs, a Black Hebrew Israelite organization in Miami, were apprehended on charges of murder, attempted murder, arson, and extortion in 1990. The Yahwehs believe that blacks, not Jews, are the true Israelites referred to in the Bible. Among the anti-white, anti-Jewish statements in Yahweh newsletters was: "This white man with his tricks must be removed."

Ironically, white separatists and black separatists are basically in agreement on the point that blacks and whites should not live together. It is important to acknowledge that people like Hulon Mitchell, Jr. (the leader of the Yahwehs) are just as guilty as white supremacist groups of keeping the flame of racial hatred burning.

❖ HATRED IN SCHOOL ❖

Allison knew that a group of kids in her school liked to hang out in the hallway at school during free periods and pick on boys who wore Jewish skull-caps, or yarmulkes. The Jewish boys were taunted, called names, and sometimes were even beaten up. "Basically, to be in the group, you have

Jews have often been the victims of hate crimes.

to prove that you're cool by beating up a Jewish kid," Allison says. "That's what the group does for fun."

Gangs of people may provoke violence against other groups of people who they have decided are their enemies. If you see this happening, think about what the reason might be. Just as with white supremacist groups, people may join other kinds of hate groups because they are angry and dissatisfied with their own lives, and they blame this on other people.

❖ HATE GROUPS AROUND THE WORLD ❖

The United States is not the only country that has hate groups. In Germany today, hate groups are becoming more of a problem. High unemployment in that country has made some people angry, and they have tried to blame the problem on the new immigrants who are coming to Germany. This fear and hatred of foreigners is called xenophobia. In 1991, hundreds of people marched against racist violence in Germany after the homes of some Turkish immigrants were burned down.

Germany was the home of one of the world's best-known hate groups: the Nazis, who, led by Adolf Hitler, ruled Germany from 1933 to 1945 and killed Jews, Gypsies, homosexuals, foreigners, disabled people, mentally ill, and others, in their determination to create a perfect Aryan society. While he was in prison in 1924, Hitler wrote a book called *Mein Kampf* ("My Struggle") in which he blamed Germany's problems on Jews and Communists. Hitler also wrote in *Mein Kampf* that using terror and force was the best way to gain control over people. The book was Hitler's statement of intent and the reign of terror was carried out a decade later.

In Brazil, there is also hate group violence. A gay rights group in Rio has identified twelve "extermination groups" which target gay people.

People around the world are fighting the hatred resulting from racism and hate groups. This anti-racism demonstration took place in Rome.

There is a skinhead group in Sao Paulo, Brazil with T-shirts that say "Death to Homosexuals."

Skinheads are in Sweden, too. Sweden has many immigrant workers, and this has caused resentment among some people. At a soccer tournament skinheads tried to get new members by passing out information and offering haircuts for two dollars.

❖ HOW DO PEOPLE JOIN? ❖

David Duke, a former high-ranking Ku Klux Klan leader who was elected to the Louisiana House of Representatives, has been able to bring many new followers like Tom Martinez into the Klan because he is well-dressed and articulate. Sometimes hate group leaders will tone down their message for the media in order to appear reasonable. They claim they are only being patriotic and they are trying to save America. James Farrands, the leader of the Invisible Empire of the Ku Klux Klan, says, "We don't hate anybody. We just love white people." So why have members of Farrands' group been convicted of several violent crimes, and why does he carry a loaded revolver?

Hate groups attract new members through the media. They use public-access cable TV, computer bulletin board services and recorded phone message. They also invite people to rallies and demonstrations.

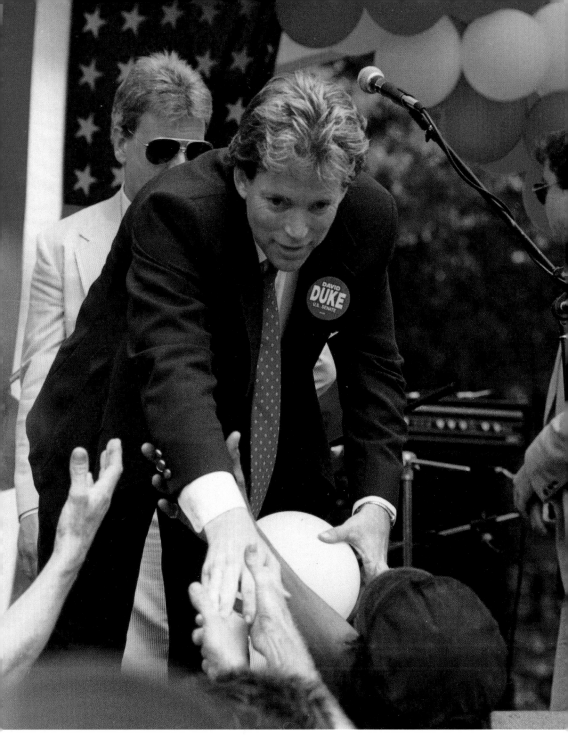

Louisiana State Representative David Duke is the head of the National Association for the Advancement of White People, former grand wizard of the Knights of the Ku Klux Klan, and in his youth, wore a swastika.

Hate groups sometimes use students to recruit other students.

❖ HATE GROUPS IN SCHOOLS ❖

Recruiting goes on in schools, too. At middle schools and high schools around the United States, hate groups are spreading their message through pamphlets and posters and, sometimes by word of mouth, through students themselves. In North Carolina, a hate group advertised to young people that they should call certain phone numbers to harass people. A woman who worked with AIDS patients received hundreds of harassing phone calls. Police and investigators were able to find out that almost all of the calls had been made by young people who had gotten the woman's phone number from hate group literature at school.

In Madison County, Georgia, in 1986, the Ku Klux Klan tried to become active in local public schools. They handed out Klan literature on school buses, held demonstrations near the school, and even shouted to students going to or from school. Parents became angry and decided to go to court. They were able to prove that the Klan was terrorizing their children and making it difficult for them to be in school. The court said that the Klan could not come within five hundred feet of the schools.

❖ QUESTIONS TO ASK YOURSELF ❖

Acts of hate happen nearly every day. You might try keeping track of newspaper or magazine articles about them. Here are some topics you could look for in those articles. 1) What kinds of hate groups are there? 2) Which ones make the news the most often? 3) Klanwatch is one organization that keeps track of hate groups and their activities. Do you think there are others? How can you find out?

chapter

3

THE PEOPLE BEHIND HATE GROUPS

KEVIN WALKED DOWN THE SCHOOL HALLWAY, *almost afraid to look at the math quiz he held in his hand. He'd missed a lot of classes and he had a feeling that the test hadn't gone so well. When he finally looked at it, his fears were confirmed. He had received a D.*

His disappointment and anger brewing inside him, Kevin stopped to look out the window. Off in the distance he could see the football team practicing. This was the last thing he needed to see. He hadn't made the team this year, even though he'd worked hard all summer getting in shape. To his left, in the school courtyard, Kevin saw a group of students who were selling egg rolls and wontons as part of a Chinese New Year celebration. Kevin recognized some of the kids from his math class. "I bet they did well on the test," he fumed. "The Asian kids always mess up the curve."

As he thought about the Asian students and how they had messed up his math score, Kevin suddenly

Hate groups, like Neo-Nazis, give their members a sense of structure and a feeling of belonging.

came up with an explanation for why he hadn't made the football team either. He was white; many of the football players were black. "The coaches like black players better!" he thought angrily. It seemed like all of Kevin's problems could be blamed on someone else.

He thought of his friend Alex, who dressed like a Skinhead and talked about "white power." "That's the idea," Kevin thought. "If whites were respected around here, I'd be a lot better off." As soon as he got home, he decided, he would call Alex to talk about joining his group.

❖ FAMILY PROBLEMS ❖

Hate group members are of various ages, backgrounds, and beliefs. But people who study hate groups believe that members' reasons for joining a hate group may be fairly predictable. Young people in particular may want the structure and attention they receive as hate group members. Perhaps they come from families where they never received much attention, or where they had no role model to give them guidance. Hate group membership gives them a sense of belonging, and the hate group falsely teaches them that they are superior to others because they are white. In addition, the militaristic structure of many hate groups provides youths with a sense of power and belonging. Hate group members may have experienced situations of domestic violence at home, where they learned to accept that violence towards others was a way to act out anger.

Floyd Cochran, a former high-ranking member of the Aryan Nations group, described how his group was able to recruit many suburban white youths. "They joined the white supremacist movement looking for a family and a place to belong. They grew up without being taught responsibility or accountability. When they came to Aryan Nations they were given a structure and told what to do. We gave them a uniform and some patches to wear. After a

while some of them would get a title and some authority."

❖ LOW SELF-ESTEEM AND SCAPEGOATING ❖

People who feel the need to look down on others who are different from themselves are basically unhappy with themselves and their own lives. Morris Dees, Executive Director of the Southern Poverty Law Center, describes typical hate group members as "life's losers." They may have trouble getting a good job, taking care of their families, or maintaining stable relationships. They seek out something to blame for their problems. When someone tells them that Jews, blacks, or homosexuals cause problems in society, they listen. This desire to place blame on someone else is called scapegoating, and it is what keeps hate groups in business.

"I couldn't find work that paid a living wage. This infuriated me: blacks and other minorities, I heard, if they wanted jobs, got them for the asking. Never once did it occur to me that perhaps the real reason I couldn't find a decent job was that I was a tenth-grade dropout." This is how former white supremacist Tom Martinez describes how he blamed others for his problems. He was watching television one night when he saw an interview with David Duke, a high-ranking leader in the Ku Klux Klan. "As Duke was talking of how the government had money to bus black kids to school but not a penny for the working-class white man, I thought, 'Damn, this guy is right. This guy is right! Who is this guy?' " Martinez wrote to Duke, who sent him an application for membership in the Klan. Martinez was excited at the chance to belong to something, and even more excited at the power he felt as a Klan member.

Hate groups are frightening because of their power to appeal to people like Tom Martinez, people for whom racism and hatred are the only things that make them feel important. Hate groups are able to convince many people that their problems are caused by minorities, Jews, or homosexuals, and that if these groups are eliminated, their problems will be solved.

❖ BEWARE OF STEREOTYPES ❖

We must be careful not to assume that we know what the typical hate group member looks like, however. Some racists let their hair grow long. Hate group members are not all from small towns in the south of the United States, nor are they all working-class white men. Some are women; some are educated; and they live all over the country, and the world. A man named William L. Pierce was both a physics professor at Oregon State University—and the head of the American Nazi Party. Hate group members may hold respectable jobs, or even public

office. David Duke, for example, served in the Louisiana state legislature.

Although the KKK started in the American South, today hate groups have spread across the country. In fact, the state with the most hate groups is California, followed by Florida, Illinois, and Pennsylvania.

❖ QUESTIONS TO ASK YOURSELF ❖

It is impossible to tell a member of a hate group simply by looking at someone. Let's think about some of the indications that someone might belong to a hate group. 1) Studies have shown that the people who join hate groups often have low self-esteem. What other characteristics might they have? 2) What symbols tend to indicate an involvement with a hate group?

chapter

4

THE YOUNG HATE-GROUP GENERATION

RACIST SKINHEADS BELONG TO A GROUP THAT began in England in the 1970s and then spread to the United States in the late 1980s.

It is estimated that there are about 3,000 Skinheads in thirty-four states. The Skinhead movement is a youth movement; most members are between the ages of fifteen and twenty-five. In fact, much organizing of Skinheads takes place in high schools. Skinheads are distinguished by their unique appearance. They sport shaved heads, swastika tattoos, and steel-toed boots. These boots, as well as baseball bats, are among the weapons Skinheads use to attack their victims. They have been known to attack Asians, Indians, Hispanics, blacks, Jews, gays, and liberal whites, as well as other Skinheads from rival gangs. Their attacks are known for being especially brutal, like the murder of Mulugeta Seraw in Portland.

Skinheads are making a name for themselves

The number of neo-Nazi skinheads is rising throughout the world. These German Skinheads raised their fists in a facist salute during a right-wing demonstration in Leipzig, Germany.

because of their extreme levels of violence. They have been shown to be responsible for twenty-eight deaths since 1987. The Anti-Defamation League of B'nai B'rith calls them the most violent of all white supremacist groups.

❖ HATE MUSIC: SKINHEAD ROCK ❖

Skinheads have their own type of music. It is called "White Power" or "Oi" music, and most of it comes from Germany or Britain. Oi music is a hard-driving type of rock music with lyrics that spread the Skinhead message of hate and violence. Oi music is a kind of Skinhead propaganda, or a way of telling people about their cause. In fact, unlike other hate groups which publish their own newspapers and magazines, Skinheads rely on their music for communication. Skinhead meetings often mean that a group of Skinheads gather at someone's house or at a club to listen to oi music.

Here is what some oi music lyrics say:

Massive inflation by the racial infestation
Has turned our streets to decay,
Racial domination, swift termination
Has become the only way
Close the border, start the New Order
Gather your guns, it's time to fight,
A call to arms!
Song: "A Call to Arms"
Band: Bound for Glory

Fighting in the city, it's a matter of life and death
It's as easy as black and white, you'll fight to your
*   last breath*
Song: "White Warriors"
Band: Skrewdriver

It is clear from the lyrics, and from some of the titles of songs ("White Warrior," "Fists of Steel," "Head Kicked In," "Blood and Honour") that oi music glorifies Skinhead violence. Listening to oi music gets Skinheads

excited and ready to go find their victims. Skinheads are also likely to combine drinking alcohol with listening to oi music, which makes it more likely that they will get out of control.

Strangely, the original Skinheads from England were fans of Jamaican reggae music before they became a racist group. Later, they decided that it was people from places like Jamaica who were taking their jobs away.

There are non-racist Skinheads, too, and there is also some music that is not racist. There is a group of Skinheads who are anti-racist called Skinheads Against Racist Prejudice (SHARP). This group, while offering some hope for positive change, can sometimes be just as violent as racist Skinheads. They have sometimes chosen to fight racism by getting into violent fights with racist Skinheads. This is not the way to solve the problem, however. Using violence to stop racist Skinheads just sends the message that violence is O.K. Racist Skinheads need to be shown in other ways that what they do is wrong.

❖ QUESTIONS TO ASK YOURSELF ❖

The Skinhead population is growing. Let's try to understand a little bit about the movement. 1) Do you know any Skinheads? 1) What is the philosophy of the Skinheads? 2) Why do you think teens join the Skinheads?

chapter

5

SOLVING THE PROBLEM

SOME STATES HAVE LAWS THAT RESTRICT THE activities of hate groups. For example, eighteen states have laws against burning crosses or other symbols. Sixteen states have banned the Klan and other violent groups. They are forbidden to wear hoods or masks.

Twenty-seven states have laws against hate crimes. Hate crimes are crimes motivated by prejudice and discrimination, and they can be committed by either groups or individuals. In most cases, hate crime laws increase the sentence for a crime if it can be proven that the crime was committed because of bias. For example, in Palm Beach County, Florida, in 1992, a fourteen-year-old boy was arrested for spray-painting swastikas and neo-Nazi messages on a Jewish synagogue. Because of the Florida hate crime law, the judge in the case was able to act on the problem. He did something pro-active. He not only ordered the boy to pay the

Hate groups often use vandalism to frighten people.

cost of cleaning the temple, but also to read
books about Jewish culture and the history of
Nazism. The judge also assigned the boy to
serve one hundred hours of community service
with a Jewish organization.

Some people oppose the idea of hate crime
laws. They say that people cannot be punished
for thinking racist thoughts, even if these
thoughts lead them to commit a crime. They
argue that the crime should be punished, and
not the ideas behind it. The issue of hate crime

laws has gone all the way to the Supreme Court. The Supreme Court decided in 1993 that states may have laws which impose stiffer sentences for hate crimes. The decision was based on a hate crime law in Wisconsin. This news is encouraging for people who want to stop hate groups, because it may mean that hate groups will stop and think before committing crimes.

Some state laws are useful in fighting hate groups. For example, there are laws in many states against trespassing, harassment, or touching another person in an offensive way. Somtimes hate groups can be prosecuted under these laws.

There is another way that the law can be used to counter hate groups. Sometimes people decide to sue a hate group in court. These lawsuits can be successful because it costs a great deal of money to fight a court case. The more money a hate group spends to defend themselves in court, the less money they will have to send out hate literature, hold meetings, and conduct other activities. The murder of Mulugeta Seraw in Portland led to a successful court case against Tom Metzger and his son John, who lead a group called the White Aryan Resistance. It was found that the Metzgers had encouraged Skinheads in Portland to commit acts of violence. In fact, right after the murder, Tom Metzger recorded a telephone message praising what the Skinheads had done. The Metzgers were ordered by the court to pay over twelve million dollars to the Seraw family. Tom Metzger and his son stood by while many of their possessions were auctioned off. This hurt the Metzgers' ability to continue their organizing.

One way that Klanwatch fights hate groups is by sending some of their own staff members to hate group rallies and meetings. There are also people in some hate groups who pretend to be in agreement, and report to Klanwatch on what the hate groups are doing. These people are called informants.

❖ **THE STORY OF BEULAH MAE DONALD** ❖

African-American Michael Donald, nineteen years old, was walking home from a friend's house in March, 1981 when he was kidnapped, beaten up, then lynched. Police found that his killers were Klan members. Michael's mother, Beulah Mae Donald, knew that her son's death had been an act of racism. She wanted to prove that her son had done nothing wrong. So even after her son's killers were sentenced (one man received a death sentence), she decided to sue the Ku Klux Klan itself. After an emotional trial, she won her case. The Klan was ordered to pay Mrs. Donald seven million dollars.

At the trial, the man who had killed her son broke down and cried. He said to Mrs. Donald:

"I can't bring your son back. God knows if I could trade places with him, I would. I can't. Whatever it takes—I have nothing. But I will have to do it. And if it takes me the rest of my life to pay it, for any comfort it will bring, I will."

❖ WHAT YOU CAN DO ❖

"But I'm not a police officer or a lawyer," you may be thinking. "What can I do about hate groups?"

The good news is that there is plenty that you can do. In fact, because of the growing numbers of youth who are attracted by the hate group message, it is especially important that young people are aware of the danger of hate groups and ways to stop them.

❖ LOOK AT YOURSELF ❖

You can start with yourself. You can make a better case against prejudice in others if you first stamp out prejudice in yourself. First, realize that we are all prejudiced to some extent simply because of the messages we receive from society. You may have even absorbed ideas from your family or friends. Recognizing this prejudice is an important step towards getting rid of it. This is a step that some people never take. Ask yourself some questions, such as, "How do I feel when I see a person of another race coming

Racial tensions can escalate to personal confrontation.

towards me on the street? Do I automatically
assume something about them? Do I feel
threatened?

Look at your friends and the people you
know. Do they tend to be similar to you in race,
ethnicity, or religion? Open yourself up to the
possibility of having friends who are different
from you.

A young man who was the leader of one of
the largest Nazi youth groups in the United
States described how he became a racist at
the age of thirteen when he was beaten up by
some African-American boys in his school. This
case points out the harm that can be caused
by bias incidents. If you are involved in a bias

incident, or you know of one at your school, talk to someone about it, like a teacher, school counselor, or parent. It is important to realize that bias incidents can cause lasting damage unless a victim's feelings are dealt with. The young man in this case began to hate all African-Americans after being attacked by a small group. A bias incident victim must work through feelings of hate and fear after an incident in order to overcome lasting prejudice.

❖ KNOWLEDGE IS POWER ❖

You may find it helpful to attend cultural events or read books about other cultures. The more you understand people who are different from you, the less likely you are to fear or dislike them. Did you know that scientists have found that people of the same race are actually just as different from each other as people from different races? Knowledge such as this is a weapon against racism.

Floyd Cochran, former Aryan Nations member, describes how his own lack of knowledge contributed to his racism. "In upper New York state, where I grew up, there are very few black people. I believed the usual caricatures that white people make of black people." Even if you, like Floyd Cochran, live in an area with few minorities, that does not mean that you have to stereotype people. If your school does not

already have classes about other cultures, talk to some teachers or administrators about getting some in the curriculum. The young leader of one of the largest skinhead groups in the American South says that he became a racist at the age of sixteen by reading books like *The Hoax of the Twentieth Century*, which says that the Holocaust never happened. (The Holocaust refers to the systematic persecution and destruction of millions. Jews, Gypsies, Communists, Catholics, and the mentally ill were destroyed by Hitler and the Nazis.) Realize that even though some things, like the Holocaust, may seem like obvious horrors to you, not everybody knows all the facts. While you can't be responsible for anyone else's education, you can be responsible for your own, and you can share your knowledge with others.

The Southern Poverty Law Center has a project called Teaching Tolerance which produces a magazine and videos, designed to help teachers fight prejudice in young people. The goal of the project is to increase understanding and communication among students of different backgrounds. The idea is that if we can teach young people how to get along, they will get along better as adults. The address of the Southern Poverty Law Center is in the back of this book. If your teachers have not already heard of Teaching Tolerance, suggest that they write the

One way to put an end to hatred and misunderstanding is to teach people about cultures and religions other than their own.

Southern Poverty Law Center to receive the materials, which are provided free of charge.

The Anti-Defamation League in Boston decided to attack the problem of hate crime among youths using education. They started a prejudice-awareness program called A World of Difference Institute. Youths who were convicted of hate crimes were sentenced to twenty hours of activities. There were community service projects, field trips to synagogues, and a community fair in a black neighborhood. Aaron, a student who had been found guilty of beating another student with a lead pipe while shouting racial slurs, said later: "I learned that everyone is like me in some way. This program has helped me change my views on other groups of people. It has opened my eyes."

❖ HATE GROUPS IN YOUR COMMUNITY ❖

The student who founded a group called Teens Against Racial Prejudice describes how it was students who made the community confront racism after an African-American man Tony Montgomery, was murdered by skinheads. "At my school they (adults) never talked about (Montgomery's) death . . . They didn't seem to want to deal with it as an act of racism. They didn't want to face the fact that things like this do happen in Reno." People may not want to admit that there is racism in their community.

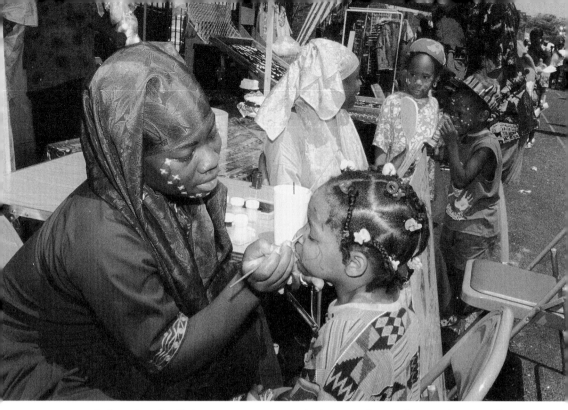

Cultural and religious events are good places to learn about other people and their beliefs.

If you believe that people are ignoring racism in your city or town, collect your evidence carefully. Watch the news and read the newspapers. Do you feel that you have been discriminated against? What about people you know?

❖ BUILD YOUR DEFENSE ❖

It is important for communities to attack the problem of racism early on, before hate groups have a chance to take advantage of bigotry that may already exist. This way, communities are better prepared to fight the hate groups if they do arrive. Remember that hate groups thrive on crises. For example, in a town in Maine, many people lost their jobs because of a company lay-off. Thinking that people would be ready to blame the problem on minorities, the Klan arrived, burned a cross, and held a rally in the town. They were surprised when they were met by a huge peaceful protest, including a Holocaust survivor's personal plea. The community had decided that they didn't want or need the Klan.

Other cases of communities saying no to the Klan have occurred throughout the country. Klanwatch reports that fear and silence are what a hate group hopes to find in a community. By working with other students and community members, you can make sure that your community is neither afraid not silent. Just because a hate group may have the legal right to march in your town doesn't mean that you have to stand by and watch them do it.

- Make posters telling the group what you think of them.
- Hold a counter-demonstration.
- Call local or national anti-hate organizations to let them know what is going on in your area. Perhaps they can help you organize your response to the hate group, or they may want to come and help out.

It's very likely that hate groups exist in your area even if you have never seen or heard of them. Remember that dealing with hate groups can be very dangerous. Your main responsibility is to stay informed and prepared. Leave the hands-on work to the proper authorities.

❖ HATE GROUPS AT YOUR SCHOOL ❖

Rita couldn't believe some of the posters that she had started seeing in the hallways of her high school. "Do you feel outnumbered?" one of the signs said, with a picture of a white student surrounded by Asian, Hispanic and African-American students. "Fight for your rights!" Rita knew that her school had many minority students, and more seemed to be coming all the time because of new immigrant families moving into her city. Yes, it was frustrating sometimes, Rita thought, that teachers sometimes had to take extra time for students who did not know English very well. Sometimes school announcements were made in Spanish and in English. And more new student clubs were popping up, like the Chinese Students' Club and the Puerto Rican Students' Club.

Rita didn't really mind these changes, but she knew that other students did. The posters Rita had begun to see in the hallways showed that some students were so upset that they had decided to form a group of their own: a white students' group. In their meetings, the students

talked about how they felt that their school had too many non-white students. But instead of talking about why they felt threatened by the new students, the white students' group talked about how much they hated them and wanted to get them out of the school. Rita had heard that some of the white students had even talked about becoming Skinheads.

❖ BE PREPARED ❖

Think about what might happen if some students at your school wanted to start a hate group, and wanted to hold their meetings on your campus. Do you know how school officials, and your fellow students, would respond? The Center for Democratic Renewal in Atlanta, Georgia recommends that schools consider what action they would take in such a situation. In some cases, schools can limit what kinds of groups meet on campus, especially if a group makes other students feel threatened or intimidated.

❖ TAKE ACTION ❖

If you already know or suspect that a student hate group meets on your campus, you can approach the problem in several ways. One way would be to challenge the group's right to meet on your school grounds. Talk to your principal, or to a teacher, about the group's beliefs and activities. If they are already causing problems in the school, or if you can prove that they are planning to cause problems, it may not be too difficult to stop them from meeting there.

Another way to approach the problem of hate groups at your school is to approach the hate group directly. Talk to the group's leaders about why they are so angry. Attend one of the group's meetings to see what they are talking about, if you feel comfortable doing so. Take a friend along. If you are made to feel uncomfortable in any way, leave the meeting and talk to an adult you trust about what happened.

❖ JOIN TOGETHER ❖

You may not feel comfortable attacking this problem on your own. Other students probably feel the same way you do, so why not ask them to join you? Together, you can start an anti-racism group. Try to have students of as many different backgrounds as possible in your group. If your school does not have to deal with a hate group on campus right now, don't give one a chance to form: you can start your own anti-hate group anyway. Some projects for your group might include: a panel of speakers about discrimination in your school or city, a Martin Luther King, Jr. Birthday march or celebration, or a multicultural film festival. If your school has a newspaper, perhaps you could even write a

Classmates can help develop tolerance by teaching each other about
their different backgrounds.

letter to the editor or an editorial column about
problems of discrimination at your school.

❖ EMPOWERING YOURSELF AGAINST RACISM ❖

What you do is important. As Christina
Davis-McCoy, executive director of North
Carolinians Against Racist and Religious
Violence, says: "It's sad that at times there has
been a sort of vacuum where students haven't
been given the opportunity to act responsibly.
Teens can play a vital role in breaking the cycle
of bigotry."

Teens have already taken the lead in some
places. Teens Against Racial Prejudice works in

the Nevada area. In Minneapolis, Minnesota, a multi-racial youth group called "Anti-Racist Action" has fought Skinheads by working together with gay and lesbian organizations and college groups.

North Carolinians Against Racist and Religious Violence (NCARRV) is an organization with an extensive youth program called "Breaking the Cycle of Bigotry." For example, since 1990 they have run a summer program for teens which brings young people together from across the state. They also go into schools to speak to students about what to do if they are facing the problems of hate groups in their school or community.

NCARRV focuses on empowering young people to take it upon themselves to fight racism. Sometimes, according to NCARRV, principals or teachers who find hate group materials or know about a hate group on campus want to ignore the issue. They are afraid that if they let other people know about the problem, the school will get a bad reputation. Of course, this will never solve the problem, and the school will get an even worse reputation in the long run. Sometimes, young people are the only ones willing to take the initiative.

❖ WRITE A LETTER ❖

In the back of this book, there is a list of national and local organizations that deal with

hate groups. Feel free to write or call the one
closest to you for advice on how to start a group
like theirs at your school. They will surely be
excited about your proposal. A letter to the
organization nearest you might look something
like this:

Your name
your address

To Whom it May Concern:

My name is_____ and I
am___ years old. I am concerned about
the possibility of hate groups in my school
and community. I know the problem of
young people joining hate groups is growing.

I understand you are involved in working against hate groups in our area. I am
very interested in helping you.

Please send me information about your
organization and how I can get involved.
Do you have information that I can pass
out to other students at my school? Would
it be possible to start a student chapter of
your organization at my school? Thank you
for your help.

Sincerely,

_____
(your name)

❖ PICK UP THE PHONE ❖

If you feel that the problem of hate groups in your school or community is urgent, you may prefer to call the organization instead of writing. First, introduce yourself. Say that you are a student and name your school and city. Say that you would like to talk to someone about hate group activity. The person who answers the phone may be an operator or secretary who will need to transfer your call to someone else. Don't give up if it is a little frustrating and confusing at first. Slow yourself down, and repeat yourself two or three times, if necessary.

Once you have the right person on the phone, explain why you are calling. Specify whether you know about a hate group in your school or community, or if you just want general information. Ask if the organization has anyone who works specifically with youth issues who could advise you about how to approach the problem in your school.

Ask the organization to send you some information, so you can learn more about what they do, as well as getting more facts about hate groups and hate crimes.

❖ STORIES OF HOPE ❖

Can people who hate ever change? Fortunately, we know that they can. The reason we know this is because there are examples of

You can make a difference in the fight against hate groups.

people who have quit hate groups and turned their lives around.

One of the most amazing stories is about Larry Trapp, a man in Lincoln, Nebraska who was a Grand Dragon in the Ku Klux Klan. A Grand Dragon is the senior leader. Trapp made many threatening phone calls to Michael and Julie Weisser, a Jewish couple. But he did not get the response he expected.

Instead of being frightened by Trapp, the

Weissers decided to befriend him. They moved him into their home and took care of him when he became sick from diabetes. When Trapp died a year later, he had quit the Klan.

Floyd Cochran's story of why he left the Aryan Nations is also amazing, because it shows how simply one can prove the stupidity of racism. Cochran was in Tennessee helping the Klan recruit new members. He showed the Klan members a picture of his two sons. The clan leader noticed that one of the boys had a cleft palate, and the leader said he would have to be killed because he was genetically imperfect.

Cochran started thinking. His son had simply been born that way. He didn't do anything wrong. Cochran realized that, like his son, people of different races and ethnicities had also done nothing wrong. Their color was something they had been born with. Cochran decided that the way he had hated had been wrong. Now, since he has quit the hate group, Cochran has become an activist against racism. He has joined the struggle for human rights.

These stories of hope show that hate group members are people who have the potential to change. People are not born with ideas of hate. They learn these ideas. You can help other people your age learn that it is wrong to hate. You can help fight hate when you see it in your school or community. Hate has a long history

around the world. But if we all work on this problem together, we can make hate a thing of the past. Martin Luther King, Jr., said: "Injustice anywhere is a threat to justice everywhere."

Maybe you feel what you do in your school or community doesn't really matter to the rest of the world. But it does. Every small step brings us closer to the goal of justice for eveyone, everywhere.

❖ QUESTIONS TO ASK YOURSELF ❖

The issue of hate groups has been addressed on many levels. Let's think about what has been done, and what there is to be done. 1) What action has been taken on state and federal levels to end hate crimes? 2) Why can't hate groups be outlawed? 3) Are you prejudiced? In what way? How can you eliminate prejudice in yourself? 4) What action can you take to help combat racism and hate crimes?

GLOSSARY

aryan Hitler used the word to define his phony master race. To avoid this bad meaning, we now call this group of people Indo-Europeans.

bigotry Prejudice, intolerance. Bigots are so attached to their own ideas that they cannot tolerate anyone else's.

ethnic origin A person's cultural and racial background.

Latino Generally used to refer to Spanish-speaking U.S. residents.

Nazis The National Socialist German Workers Party, led to power in Germany by Adolf Hitler.

Neo-nazi Organizations or individuals who follow in the footsteps of the original German Nazi Party. Neo means new.

prejudice A judgement or opinion formed before any information is gathered.

race Rejected by anthropologists as a meaningless biological concept, but still widely used to categorize human beings.

racist As a noun, an individual or group who base their hatred of other people, on race. Also as an adjective: racist idea, racist book, etc.

white Generally refers to people of European descent.

white supremacy A false concept of superiority.

xenophobia Hatred of foreign people. Phobia means fear.

ORGANIZATIONS TO CONTACT

Anti-Defamation League of B'nai B'rith
823 United Nations Plaza
New York, NY 10017
(212) 490-2525

Break the Silence (Coalition Against Anti-Asian Violence)
P.O. Box 2165
San Francisco, CA 94126
(415) 982-2959

Center for Democratic Renewal
P.O. Box 50469
Atlanta, GA 30302
(404) 221-0025
Midwest Office: P.O. Box 413767
Kansas City, MO 64141-3767
(816) 421-6614

Coalition for Human Dignity
P.O. Box 40344
Portland, OR 97240
(503) 281-5823

Community United Against Violence
514 Castro St.
San Francisco, CA 94114
(415) 864-3112

Klanwatch Project
Southern Poverty Law Center
P.O. Box 548
Montgomery, AL 36101-0548
(205) 264-0268

**The National Gay and Lesbian Task Force/
    Anti-Violence Project**
1734 14th St., N.W.
Washington D.C. 20009-4309
(202) 332-6483

**National Institute Against Prejudice and
    Violence**
31 South Greene St.
Baltimore, MD 21201
(301) 328-5170

Neighbors Network
1544 Piedmont Ave. #73
Atlanta, GA 30324
(404) 257-5550

**North Carolinians Against Racism and
    Religious Violence**
P.O. Box 240
Durham, NC 27702
(919) 688-5965

People Against Racist Terror
P.O. Box 1990
Burbank, CA 91507
(310) 288-5003

ORGANIZATIONS IN CANADA

B'nai Brith Canada
15 Hove Street
Downsview, ON M3H4Y8
(416) 633-6224

Canadian Council for Racial Harmony
PO Box 190
Station J
Toronto, ON M4J4Y1

Center for Research-Action on Race Relations
#220, 1650 Berri
Montreal, PQ H2L 4E6
(514) 843-3892

Multiculturalism and Citizenship Canada
Ottawa, ON K1A 0M5
(819) 997-0055

FOR FURTHER READING

Applebome, Peter. "Skinhead Violence Grows, Experts Say." *New York Times*, July 18, 1993.

Bullard, Sara, Ed. *The Ku Klux Klan: A History of Racism and Violence*. Montgomery, Alabama: Klanwatch, 1991.

Center for Democratic Renewal. *When Hate Groups Come to Town: A Handbook of Effective Community Responses*. Montgomery, Alabama: Black Belt Press, 1992.

Grunsell, Angela. *Let's Talk About Racism*. New York: Gloucester Press, 1991.

Gysin, Catherine. "Young White Racists." *Sassy*, March 1989.

Klanwatch Project of the Southern Poverty Law Center. *Hate, Violence, and White Supremacy*. Montgomery, Alabama, 1989.

Osborn, Kevin. *Tolerance*, rev. ed. New York: Rosen Publishing Group, 1993.

Palmer, Ezra, *Everything You Need to Know About Discrimination*, rev. ed. New York: Rosen Publishing Group, 1993.

Sherman, William. "The Boys in the Hoods." *Mirabella*, September 1992, pp. 144–150.

Sounds of Hate: Neo-Nazi Rock Music from Germany. New York: Anti-Defamation League, 1992.

INDEX

64

HATE GROUPS

ABOUT THE AUTHORS

Rose Blue is a freelance writer whose credits include nearly thirty books for children and young adults, both fiction and nonfiction. She is also contributing editor and feature writer for *Teacher Magazine*, as well as consultant for several other periodicals.

Ms. Blue resides in Brooklyn, New York.

Corinne J. Naden works as a freelance writer, editor, and copy editor. She is the author of twenty-six nonfiction books for young adults, librarians, and teachers.

Ms. Naden lives in Dobbs Ferry, New York.

PHOTO CREDITS: AP/Wide World Photos
PHOTO RESEARCH: Vera Amadzadeh
RESEARCH AND EDITING: Jennifer Croft
DESIGN: Kim Sonsky